T0128949

QUOTES, THOUGHTS, AND OTHER GENERAL NONSENSE THAT COMES INTO MY HEAD

JEFF IRELAND

authorHOUSE®

AuthorHouse™
1663 Liberty Drive
Bloomington, IN 47403
www.authorhouse.com
Phone: 1 (800) 839-8640

© 2018 Jeff Ireland. All rights reserved.

No part of this book may be reproduced, stored in a retrieval system, or transmitted by any means without the written permission of the author.

Published by AuthorHouse 08/25/2018

ISBN: 978-1-5462-2083-1 (sc)
ISBN: 978-1-5462-2082-4 (e)

Library of Congress Control Number: 2017918898

Print information available on the last page.

Any people depicted in stock imagery provided by Thinkstock are models, and such images are being used for illustrative purposes only. Certain stock imagery © Thinkstock.

This book is printed on acid-free paper.

Because of the dynamic nature of the Internet, any web addresses or links contained in this book may have changed since publication and may no longer be valid. The views expressed in this work are solely those of the author and do not necessarily reflect the views of the publisher, and the publisher hereby disclaims any responsibility for them.

Scripture taken from The Holy Bible, King James Version. Public Domain

Scripture quotations marked NIV are taken from the Holy Bible, New International Version®. NIV®. Copyright © 1973, 1978, 1984 by International Bible Society. Used by permission of Zondervan. All rights reserved. [Biblica]

Dedication

Ashley
Kayla
Sam

Introduction

Well you now are holding my quote book that I am pretty sure virtually nobody will read it cover to cover. It is actually better to have a calendar than a book for daily quotes. With that said I am a self-publisher and the company I publish with does not do calendars for your desk or end table. I certainly hope you pick this up once and awhile and check out the day you are in at that moment our maybe a birthday or anniversary. There are a couple of points I would like to make. This book was well at least in consecutive years, six years in the making. I received a nice leather-bound book at a business meeting I attended with all blank pages. In the front cover, I put "quotes, thoughts, and other general nonsense that comes into my mind" I jotted in this for over six years. Additionally, there are several quotes I discovered going through old files that are literally from over 30 years ago. The quotes that I wrote in the book are noted they are from thoughts that hit me on and off over the years. Many of my quotes are in acronym form, those you will find a statement at top of the page and the word underlined and the acronym going vertical below the statement. An example is in June the acronym called BOLD GUTS days as each letter has three important points (30 years ago). You will also discover quickly that I am person of faith so you will find many bible verses and faithful thoughts as well. The picture on the back of the book, well yes that is me at the age of six. I thought it was a good indication of where all your learning in life starts and if you are wise you will understand learning should never stop. My library at home has over 400 books in it on pretty much any topic you would like to mention that I have read and it will continue to grow. This one is now there and yes, I am extremely proud of it. The way I view it, this project was a life time in the making.

I truly hope you enjoy some of the thoughts and quotes that you run across!

Jeff Ireland

"THE LORD GETS HIS BET SOLDIERS OUT OF THE HIGHLIGHTS OF AFFLICTION."

CHARLES HADDON SPURGON

IF YOU WANT TO FIND HAPPINESS IN LIFE...
"IT COMES FROM LOOKING FOR HOW
YOU CAN HELP OTHERS AND THEN...
DELIVER THAT NEED OR SERVICE!"

JI

WHEN YOU START A PROJECT...
"BEGIN WITH THE END IN MIND
THEN DEVELOP YOUR PLAN ON
HOW TO EXECUTE IT,
THEN FOLLOW THROUGH WITH THE PLAN!"

JI

UNDERSTAND WHAT BRINGS IT TO YOU IS...

"IF YOU ARE HOPEFUL, CONFIDENT AND
CHEERFUL IN LIFE YOU ATTRACT <u>SUCCESS!</u>"

JI

"ISN'T IT FUNNY HOW DAY BY DAY NOTHING CHANGES, BUT WHEN YOU LOOK BACK EVERYTHING IS DIFFERENT!"

JI

UNDERSTAND WHAT <u>ACRONYM</u> MEANS...
ALWAYS
CONSIDER
REAL
OPPORTUNITY
NOW (ON)
YOUR
MISSION

JI

"LOVE THE LORD, YOUR GOD WITH ALL YOUR HEART AND WITH ALL YOUR SOUL AND WITH ALL YOUR STRENGTH"

DEUTERONOMY

6 : 5

ALWAYS BELIEVE...

"AS YOU GO THROUGH LIFE ALONG THE WAY
ASK YOURSELF: IF WHAT YOU ARE DOING
TODAY IS GOING TO GET YOU CLOSER TO
WHERE YOU WANT TO BE IN THE FUTURE
YOU SHOULD ALWAYS FOLLOW YOUR DREAM!"

JI

IN LIFE UNDERSTAND THIS ABOUT <u>HOPE</u>...

HARD
OBSTACLES
PASS
EVENTUALLY

JI

"I'LL TAKE GOOD LUCK OVER GOOD SKILL
ANY DAY OF THE WEEK!"

JI

"BE KIND AND COMPASSIONATE TO ONE
ANOTHER, FORGIVING EACH OTHER, JUST AS
IN CHRIST GOD FORGAVE YOU"

EPHESIANS
4 : 32

"THE CHARIOT OF FIRE DOES NOT HAVE A
REVERSE GEAR!"

JI

<u>LIVING</u> WITH JOY WHEN YOU ARE...

LOVING
INTELLIGENCE
VALUING
INTEGRITY
NEAR
GOD

JI

NO MATTER THE SITUATION, NEVER LET YOUR EMOTIONS OVERPOWER YOUR INTELLIGENCE!

JI

THE HARDEST SKILL TO MASTER...

"LEARNING TO SEE THINGS AS
THEY ARE, NOT AS YOU WANT
THEM TO BE!"

JI

YOU DEVELOP YOUR <u>SYSTEM</u>...

SETTING
YOUR
SUCCESS
THROUGH
EMOTIONAL
MOTIVATION

JI

"YOU WILL SEE AS YOU GO THROUGH
LIFE THAT BY IN LARGE,
LIFE THAT BY IN LARGE,

EMOTIONAL PEOPLE MAKE BAD DECISIONS!"

JI

"NOT GETTING WHAT YOU WANT IS
SOMETIMES A WONDERFUL STROKE OF
LUCK!"

Chinese Fortune Cookie

MAN-CAVE OF SUCCESS...

**MENTAL
ATTITUDE
NECESSARY (TO)
CREATE
A
VISION
ENTHUSIASTICALLY**

JI

"AS YOU GO THROUGH LIFE IT IS SOMETIMES HARD TO BE POSITIVE UNDERSTAND IT IS IMPORTATNT TO ALWAYS BELIEVE YOU CAN MAKE A DIFFERENCE IN WHAT YOU BRING WITH YOUR TALENT THAT THE LORD GAVE YOU..."

JI

MAN-FROG

MENTAL
ATTITUDE
NECESSARY
FULLY
RELY
ON
GOD

"DON'T LOOK BACK A LOT ONCE YOU LEARNED A LESSON FROM THE EXPERIENCE AS YOU ARE NOT GOING THAT WAY AS YOU GO FORWARD!"

JI

"FOR GOD SENT NOT HIS SON INTO THE WORLD TO CONDEMN THE WORLD; BUT THAT THE WORLD THROUGH HIM MIGHT BE SAVED."

JOHN
3 : 17

HOW TO DRIVE YOUR CAREER...

"WHEN YOU REACH THE EXTRA
MILE IN EFFORT...
HIT THE GAS - NO TRAFFIC JAM THERE!"

JI

"HE THAT IS GOOD FOR MAKING EXCUSES IS SELDOM GOOD FOR ANYTHING ELSE!"

BENJAMIN FRANKLIN (1706 – 1790)

"WHEN RUNNING A TEAM YOU SHOULD ALWAYS KEEP YOUR EYE OPEN AND CATCH PEOPLE DOING THINGS RIGHT, THEN RECOGNIZE THEM FOR THEIR POSITVE ACTION AND EFFORT FOR THE TEAM… IN FRONT OF THE TEAM…"

JI

THE DREAM

KEEP YOUR EYES FOCUSED,
LOOKING TOWARD THE SKY,
IF YOU DO YOU WILL SELDOM
EXPLAIN OR ASK WHY.
THE ADVERSITY AND STRIFE
THAT WILL SURELY STOP BY,
WILL BE GONE AND SKIPPED OVER
IN THE BLINK OF AN EYE.

MERRILY USED TO TELL US THAT
LIFE IS BUT A DREAM
THE OLDER YOU GET THE FASTER IT
GOES, OR SO IT WOULD SEEM.
SO, MAKE EACH DAY COUNT TOWARD
YOUR FANTASTIC SCHEME
TO MAKE LIFE AS GRAND AS YOU CAN
WITH PRIDE & SELF ESTEEEM.

TIME RUNS AWAY SO SLOWLY,
YET WALKS AWAY SO FAST
YOU CAN'T BUILD A FUTURE
LIVING IN YOUR PAST.
STAY FOCUSED ON WHAT'S AHEAD
AND YOUR VISION SO GRAND,
FOR WHEN YOUR MEMORIES ARE
GREATER THAT YOUR DREAMS,
LIFE GETS DIFFICULT TO STAND.

SO, SET YOUR GOALS AND
BELIEVE IN YOURSELF
AS YOU GO ROWING DOWN THE STREAM.
ALWAYS BE BRAVE AND VERY BOLD
AND MAKE YOURS THE BIGGEST DREAMS.

JI

"VISUALIZE"

YOUR MIND DOES NOT KNOW...
THAT YOUR BODY IS NOT DOING IT!

FIGURE THIS OUT ABOUT YOUR TALENT...

1) WHAT KNOWLEDGE DO YOU OWN?
2) WHAT MAKES YOU DIFFERENT?
3) WHAT MAKES YOU RELEVANT?

JI

"JESUS GIVE ME THE GRACE TO TRUST IN YOU TODAY"

ACTS
14 : 19

3 STEP PROCESS IN SELLING...

1) START WITH AN ITINERARY
2) SET AN AGENDA ON WHAT TO ACCOMPLISH
3) RECAP THE MEETING AND FOLLOW UP ON THE RECAP

JI

HOW DO YOU THINK ABOUT WORRY?

WILL
OBSTACLES
REALLY
REVERSE
YOU

JI

"SELF FORGIVENESS IS INCREDIBLY
POWERFUL...
YOU CANNOT ENJOY PEACE OF MIND
UNTIL...
YOU MAKE PEACE WITH YOURSELF!"

JI

"YOU MAY KNOW FAR LESS THAN A LOT OF PEOPLE! HOWEVER, YOU KNOW QUITE A BIT MORE THAN MOST, ALWAYS BELIEVE IN YOURSELF!"

JI

EFFORTS FOR SUCCEEDING!

"MAKE YOUR VISION CLEAR…
MAKE YOUR PLAN SIMPLE…
MAKE YOUR EFFORTS FOCUSED…
MAKE YOUR FOUNDATION STRONG!"

JI

IF IT CROSSES YOUR MIND AS YOU LEAVE
THE HOUSE TAKE IT WITH YOU...
"BETTER TO HAVE IT AND NOT NEED IT
THAN NEED IT AND NOT HAVE IT!"

JI

BIBLE

BASIC
INSTRUCTION
BEFORE
LEAVING
EARTH

STANDARD QUESTIONS...

1) DO YOU LIKE YOUR JOB?
2) DO YOU LIKE YOUR BOSS?
3) DO YOU GET PAID ENOUGH?
ALWAYS REMEMBER THIS FACT...

"WE ALL GET PAID THE SAME – 1,440 MINUTES A DAY, IT IS WHAT YOU DO WITH THAT TIME THAT MAKES THE DIFFERENCE IN YOUR LIFE!"

JI

SALES CALL AND PROJECT FOLLOW UP PLAN...

WHO DOES
WHAT,
BY WHEN?

YOU SHOULD SAY TO YOURSELF....

I AM!

"A SELF-STARTER, WHO IS DISCIPLINED, FOCUSED, DEPENDABLE, ENERGETIC, PERSON. A PERSISTENT POSITIVE THINKER WHO APPRECIATES THE OPPORTUNITY ANY COMPANY GIVES ME!"

JI

"BE PATIENT; IN TIME, EVEN AN EGG WILL WALK!"

DALAI LAMA

Q-TIP

QUIT
TAKING
IT
PERSONAL

"THE CARROT ALWAYS WINS OVER THE STICK… ASK THE HORSE!"

JI

THE WAY YOU SHOULD LOOK AT THINGS...

IS IT **T**RUE?
IS IT **H**ELPFUL?
IS IT **I**NSPIRING?
IS IT **N**ECESSARY?
IS IT **K**IND?

JI

"YOUR ATTITUDE IS CENTRAL TO EVERYTHING IN THE SPHERE OF LIFE THAT YOU OCCUPY!"

JI

"AS WE TALK AND GET TO KNOW
EACH OTHER YOU SHOULD NOT
JUDGE MY STORY BY THE CHAPTER
IN MY LIFE YOU WALKED IN ON,
THERE WAS AN AWFUL LOT THAT HAPPENED
BEFORE WE MET…"

JI

SEVEN MOST IMPORTANT
WORDS IN SELLING...
IF YOU FOLLOW THROUGH!
"I DON'T KNOW BUT I WILL FIND OUT!"

JI

"BELIEVE NONE OF WHAT YOU HEAR AND ONLY HALF OF WHAT YOU SEE!"

BENJAMIN FRANKLIN (1706 – 1790)

"YOUR VISION WILL BECOME CLEAR WHEN YOU LOOK INSIDE YOUR HEART!"

JI

INTERVIEW STRATEGY CALLED S.O.A.R.

S - EXPLAIN THE SITUATION YOU WERE IN
THAT WAS RELATIVE TO THE QUESTION!
O - OBSTACLES YOU FACED IN THE
SITUATION!
A – ACTIONS YOU TOOK TO OVERCOME THE
SITUATION!
R – RESULTS THAT YOU RECEIVED BY THE
ACTION YOU TOOK IN THE SITUATION!

--------**DILLARD TOOTER**--------

THE PROFESSORS 18 THOUGHTS IN THE MENTIAL GAME OF GOLF TO REMEMBER IN LIFE!!

HOLES 1 – 2 - 3

THREE THOUGHTS IN LIFE THAT, ONCE GONE, NEVER COME BACK!

1. – TIME
2. - WORDS
3. – OPPORTUNITY

HOLES 4 – 5 – 6

THREE THINGS IN LIFE THAT, CAN DESTROY A PERSON!

4. - ANGER
5. - PRIDE
6. - UNFORGIVENESS

JI

THE PROFESSORS 18 THOUGHTS IN THE MENTIAL GAME OF GOLF TO REMEMBER IN LIFE!!

HOLES 7 – 8 – 9

**THREE THINGS IN LIFE THAT,
<u>YOU SHOULD NEVER LOSE</u>!**

7. - FAITH
8. - HOPE
9. - HONESTY

HOLESS 10 – 11 - 12

**THREE THINGS IN LIFE THAT,
<u>ARE MOST VALUABLE</u>!**

10. - FAITH
11. - FAMILY
12. – LOVE

JI

THE PROFESSORS 18 THOUGHTS IN THE MENTIAL GAME OF GOLF TO REMEMBER IN LIFE!!

HOLES 13 – 14 - 15

THREE THINGS IN LIFE THAT,
<u>ARE NEVER CERTAIN</u>!

13. - FORTUNE
14. - SUCCESS
15. - DREAMS

HOLES 16 – 17 - 18

THREE THINGS IN LIFE THAT,
<u>YOU SHOULD ALWAYS BE GRATEFUL FOR</u>!

16. - ADVENTURE
17. - ABUNDANCE
18. - LOVE

JI

"IT DOESN'T MAKE MUCH SENSE THAT
COMMON SENSE DOESN'T SEEM TO MAKE
ANY SENSE ANYMORE!"

JI

"YOU WILL FIND ON YOUR JOURNEY
THROUGH TIME THAT <u>YOUR</u> CHOICES…
DETERMINE WHO YOU WILL BECOME
FAR MORE THAN YOUR ABILITIES
IN WHAT YOU DO!"

JI

"WE ARE WHAT WE REPEATEDLY DO.
EXCELLENCE, THEN, IS NOT AN ACT, BUT A
HABIT!"

ARISTOTLE

"DARE TO DREAM, HOPE, BELIEVE, SEEK, FEEL, FIND AND LOVE, THAT IS WHAT BRINGS… SELF SATISFACTION!"

JI

"LIFE IS NOT A MATTER OF HOLDING GOOD CARDS, BUT SOMETIMES PLAYING A POOR HAND WELL!"

JACK LONDON (1916-1976)

"REGARDLESS OF YOUR PASSION AND THE JOURNEY YOU ARE ON WITH LIFE, TO GET TO THE TOP THERE IS NO ELEVATOR TO TAKE YOU THERE. THE HIGHER YOU WANT TO GO TO SUCCEED, THE MORE STAIRS YOU WILL HAVE TO CLIMB!

JI

LEARN HOW TO BE A FUN-FAN...
FOCUS
UNDERSTANDING (YOUR)
NEEDS... (THEN YOU)
FULLY
APPRECIATE
NOW

JI *and Ashley*

"I HAVE DISCOVERED IN LIFE, THAT YOU CAN LEARN AS MUCH FROM PEOPLE YOU WOULD LIKE TO EMULATE, AS YOU CAN LEARN FROM PEOPLE THAT YOU WOULD NOT WANT TO!"

JI

WHEN YOU DO THIS IT IS MORE FUN FINDING LOVE...

LIVE
OPTIMISTIC
VISIONS
ENTHUSIASTICALLY

JI

PRACTICE THIS AND YOU WILL WIN
IN LIFE DISCOVERING <u>FAITH</u>...

FIND
ANSWERS
IN
THE
HEART

JI

"IF YOU ARE SMART YOU WILL FIND
AS YOU AGE THAT MATURITY IS
DEALING WITH REALITY...
IN A CONSTRUCTIVE WAY!"

JI

THE GIFT YOU GIVE YOURSELF
WILL MAKE OTHERS HAPPY...

GOOD
INTENTION
FOR
TODAY

JI

LEARN TO NOT BE AFRIAD OF FUR...

FEAR OF... **F**AILURE
FEAR OF... **U**NKNOWN
FEAR OF... **R**EJECTION

JI

GOD HAS A DIFFERENT VIEW AND YOU WILL LEARN THAT ...

"A STRANGE PARADOX IN LIFE TO FINDING TRUE PERSONAL HAPPINESS, IS THAT YOU NEED TO HELP OTHER PEOPLE!"

JI

"WE SHOULD EMULATE TURTLES TO A DEGREE... THEY ONLY MAKE PROGRESS AND MOVE FORWARD WHEN THEY STICK THEIR NECK OUT!"

JI

UNDERSTND HOW TO LOOK AT YOUR DAY...

"YOU CAN'T SAVE TIME...
YOU CAN ONLY SPEND IT DIFFERENTLY!"

JI

"THE MAN WHO MOVES A MOUNTAIN
BEGINS BY CARRYING AWAY
SMALL STONES."

CONFUCIUS

THE CHALLENGE

EVERY DAY, MORE OR LESS,
WE DECIDE ON THINGS HARD TO DO.
IT SEEMS THAT WE JUMP TO A TASK,
MAKE UP OUR MINDS, AND ACT OUT ON QUE.

FOR BETTER OR WORSE, YOU
CAN'T EVER TELL,
CRYSTAL BALLS WENT OUT YEARS AGO.
SO EVEN IF YOU LIVE BY A WISHING WELL,
IT WILL TAKE TIME BEFORE YOU KNOW.

MAYBE THAT'S THE WAY IT SHOULD BE,
SO, WE WORK HARD AND TRY TO WIN.
IF, BY CHANCE, YOU LOSE THAT TIME,
HAVE THE COURAGE TO TRY AGAIN.

FOR IF WE GOT ALL OF OUR WISHES
AND WE ALWAYS SEEMED
TO BE IN THE KNOW,
HOW COULD WE EVER HAVE A DREAM?
OR HOW WOULD WE EVER GROW?

SO, HAVE FAITH IN WHATEVER YOU DECIDE,
OUR DISAPPOINTMENTS ARE HIS
APPOINTMENTS, IT'S TRUE,
IF THINGS GO BAD, DON'T HANG YOUR HEAD
FOR GOD REALLY DOES LOVE YOU.

THE NEXT TIME YOU HAVE
A DECISION TO MAKE
THAT YOU FIND HARD AND SO CONFUSING,
LOOK INSIDE YOUR HEART, BELIEVE IN GOD,

THEN YOU CAN COUNT ON NEVER LOSING.

JI

"IF" AND "WHEN" WERE PLANTED AND "NOTHING GREW UP."

TURKISH PROVERB

THE A WORD THAT CHANGES THE G WORD...

"THE FOCUS OF SINCERE APPRECIATION
WILL HELP MAKE YOUR LIFE **A** – *G*LORY...
INSTEAD OF **A** - *G*RIND!"

JI

THE ONLY EXERCISE SOME PEOPLE GET IS ONE OF THE FOLLOWING!!

1) JUMPING TO CONCLUSIONS
2) RUNNING DOWN THEIR FRIENDS
3) SIDESTEPPING RESPONSIBILITY
4) PUSHING THEIR LUCK

JI

HOW TO FIND THE MOST JOYFUL <u>SUCCESS</u>...

SETTING
UP
CONTINUOUS
CYCLES
ENCOMPASSING
SPIRITUAL
SERVICE

JI

"MAN SAYS… YOU SHOW ME AND I WILL TRUST YOU - GOD SAYS… TRUST ME AND I WILL SHOW YOU…"

PSALMS
126 : 6

"NOTHING IS A GREATER IMPEDIMENT TO BEING ON GOOD TERMS WITH OTHERS THAN BEING ILL AT EASE WITH YOURSELF."

JI

YOU SHOULD SAY TO YOURSELF

I AM...
"A SELF-STARTER, WHO IS
DISCIPLINED, FOCUSED, DEPENDABLE,
AN ENERGETIC PERSON.
A PERSISTENT POSITIVE THINKER WHO
APPRECIATES THE OPPORTUNITY ANY
COMPANY GIVES ME!"

JI

"WHEN YOUR MEMORIES ARE
GREATER THAN YOUR DREAMS,
JOY WILL BEGIN TO FADE!"

JI

"I AM NOT ONE TO LOOK INTO THE PAST, I ALWAYS LOOK FORWARD!"

RALPH KETNER (1920 – 2016)
(FOUNDER OF FOOD LION)

"CHANGE YOUR FOCUS IN LIFE
TO WHAT YOU CAN *GIVE* …
INSTEAD OF WHAT YOU CAN *GET*!"

JI

"ONE WHO LOOKS FOR A FRIEND WITHOUT FAULTS WILL HAVE NONE."

JEWISH PROVERB

LEARN TO SAY TO YOURSELF I AM...

"AN ENERGETIC, TEAM PLAYER
THAT TAKES PRIDE IN MY WORK, MY
COMPANY, MY PERSONAL INTEGRITY.
MOST IMPORTANTLY I AM A TRUSTING,
CARING, UNDERSTANDING,
SUPPORTIVE LEADER WHO...
**LOVES MY FAITH AND FAMILY FIRST!**"

JI

"WE MAKE A LIVING BY WHAT WE GET.
WE MAKE A LIFE BY WHAT WE GIVE!"

WINSTON CHURCHILL (1874 – 1965)

UNDERSTANDING WEALTH...

"THE HIGHEST RICHES IN LIFE ARE BEYOND
THE REACHING OF MONEY!
THE RICHES ARE INDEPENDENT OF
A FINANCIAL FORTUNE...
WEALTH COMES FROM FINDING FAITH!"

JI

"DO OR DO NOT!
THERE IS NO TRY!!"

YODA

"IN MATTERS OF STYLE, SWIM WITH THE CURRENT; IN MATTERS OF PRINCIPLE STAND LIKE A ROCK!"

THOMAS JEFFERSON (1742 – 1826)

EQ = V + A X B 2
"EMOTIONAL QUOTIENT IS EQUAL TO
VISION + ATTITUDE X BELIEF" (TO THE
SECOND POWER)

JI

"BUT WITHOUT FAITH IT IS IMPOSSIBLE TO PLEASE HIM: FOR HE THAT COMETH TO GOD MUST BELIEVE THAT HE IS, AND THAT HE IS A REWARDER OF THEM THAT DILIGENTLY SEEK HIM"

HEBREWS
11 : 6

A GOOD VISION IN LIFE ...

"YOUR GREATEST AIM IN LIFE SHOULD BE TO
TAKE IN AS MUCH SWEETNESS AND BEAUTY
YOU ARE CAPABLE OF ABSORBING!"

JI

"ATTITUDES ARE THE FORERUNNERS OF
CONDITIONS – DON'T EVER FORGET IT!"

JI

CONSISTENCY IS KEY...

"THE DISCIPLINE OF THE MIND AND THE STATE OF THE HEART ARE THE SECRETS TO FINDING HAPPINESS!"

JI

"VISION WITHOUT ACTION IS A DAYDREAM.
ACTION WITHOUT VISION IS A NIGHTMARE"

JAPANESE PROVERB

"NOW FAITH IS THE SUBSTANCE OF THINGS HOPED FOR, THE EVIDENCE OF THINGS NOT SEEN"

HEBREWS
11 : 1

ODD POINT OF VIEW MOST PEOPLE CARRY...

"YOU ALWAYS SEEM TO HAVE TIME TO DO THINGS OVER, BUT NOT ENOUGH TIME TO DO IT CORRECTLY TO START WITH!"

JI

"FOLLOW THE PATH BUT PUT <u>PRIORITIES IN THE PROPER ORDER</u>; FAITH, FAMILY, FINANCE! LIFE WORKS OUT MUCH BETTER WITH THAT STRATEGY!"

JI

"YOU SHOULD ALWAYS TRY AND MAKE THE BEST EFFORT TO SURROUND YOURSELF WITH POSITIVE, SUCCESSFUL, SUPPORTIVE PEOPLE, BELIEVE ME... IT HELPS!"

JI

"IF YOU KNEW HOW POWERFUL YOUR MIND IS… YOU WOULD NEVER THINK A NEGATIVE THOUGHT AGAIN?"

JI

HOW YOU LOOK AT THINGS
IS CRITICAL IN <u>LIFE</u>...

NEGATIVE	**POSITIVE**
LIFE	LIFE
ISN'T	IS
FAIR	FULLY
EVER	EXCITING

JI

"TO HANDLE YOURSELF, USE YOU HEAD: TO HANDLE OTHERS USE YOUR HEART"

ELEANOR ROOSEVELT (1884 – 1962)

"WHEN YOU ARE HUNGRY YOU ARE HAPPY!
IF YOU LOSE HUNGER WITH SUCCESS,
OR IF YOU ARE ON TOP AND YOU ARE NOT
SURE WHERE TO GO, YOU WILL BE UNHAPPY...
*UNDERSTAND YOU MUST ALWAYS CLIMB TO
FIND JOY IN LIFE AND BE HAPPY!*"

JI

THE GIFT

I KNOW THE SECRET TO HAPPINESS,
I'VE LIVED IT FOR QUITE SOME TIME.
SEEK OUT YOUR NATURAL TALENTS
WE ALL HAVE DIFFERENT KINDS.

FOLLOW YOUR PATH BY THE
FEEL OF YOUR HEART,
AND GOD WILL SHOW YOU THE SIGNS.
PEACE AND JOY WILL COME FROM THE START,
AND THINGS WILL WORK OUT JUST FINE.

IF YOU POUR OUT YOUR SKILLS
THAT YOU HAVE BEEN GIVEN,
THE SWEAT OF YOUR BROW
FINDS THOSE IN NEED.
YOU WON'T KNOW OR CARE
WHY YOU'RE SO DRIVEN,
THE LORD'S WORK GOES ON
WITH YOU AS THE SEED.

IF YOU HELP OUT OTHERS IN THIS WAY,
AND NOT WORRY ABOUT YOUR REWARD.
THE PEACE IN YOUR MIND,
THE JOY IN YOUR HEART,
CANNOT BE BOUGHT OR SOLD.

SO, TAKE A LESSON FROM AN OLDER MAN,
DON'T GO LOOKING OUTSIDE OF YOURSELF.
FOR FULFILLMENT, LOVE, AND
TRUE SATISFACTION,
CANNOT BE BOUGHT OFF A SHELF.

BELIEVE IN YOUR FAITH,
BELIEVE IN YOURSELF,
BELIEVE IN YOUR VALUES AND DREAMS.
FOR YOU ARE TRULY ONE OF
GOD'S CHILDREN,
AND PART OF HIS BEAUTIFUL DREAM!

JI

"IF ATTITUDES WERE ON
SALE AT THE STORE...
WOULD YOU BUY YOURS?"

JI

"YOUR KIDS WILL BECOME WHAT YOU ARE SO…
BE WHAT YOU WANT THEM TO BE!"

JI

BOLD GUTS STRATEGY – 8 DAY PLAN TO IMPROVE LIFE!

ACRONYM STYLE DAY – 1

B – THIS IS BASICS

IN THE FOLLOWING ORDER!!!!

- DRESS RIGHT
- BE ON TIME
- SHOW RESPECT

JI

BOLD GUTS STRATEGY – 8 DAY PLAN TO IMPROVE LIFE!

ACRONYM STYLE DAY – 2

O – THIS IS OPTIMISM

IN THE FOLLOWING ORDER!!!!

- DON'T HAVE NEGATIVE THOUGHTS
- LOOK FOR ALL SILVER LININGS
- SPEAK TO PEOPLE POSITIVE

JI

BOLD GUTS STRATEGY – 8 DAY PLAN TO IMPROVE LIFE!

ACRONYM STYLE DAY – 3

L – THIS IS TO BE LOYAL

IN THE FOLLOWING ORDER!!!!

- TO GOD
- TO FAMILY
- TO SKILL SETS

JI

BOLD GUTS STRATEGY – 8 DAY PLAN TO IMPROVE LIFE!

ACRONYM STYLE DAY – 4

D – THIS IS TO ALWAYS BE DECISIVE

IN THE FOLLOWING ORDER!!!!

- TAKE RESPONSIBILITY
- MAKE DECISIONS
- TAKE ACTION

JI

BOLD GUTS STRATEGY – 8 DAY PLAN TO
IMPROVE LIFE!

ACRONYM STYLE DAY – 5

G – THIS IS GET UP AND GO

IN THE FOLLOWING ORDER!!!!

- WORK HARD
- PLAN AND GIVE IT 110% EFFORT
- FOCUS ON NEXT PHASE

JI

BOLD GUTS STRATEGY – 8 DAY
PLAN TO IMPROVE LIFE!

ACRONYM STYLE DAY – 6

U – THIS IS YOUR UNIQUE APPROACH

IN THE FOLLOWING ORDER!!!!

- SHOW YOUR TALENT
- FIND THE FIT
- CREATE THE POSITION

JI

BOLD GUTS STRATEGY – 8 DAY
PLAN TO IMPROVE LIFE!

ACRONYM STYLE DAY – 7

T – THIS IS TENACITY

IN THE FOLLOWING ORDER!!!!

- GIVE ENERGY
- KEEP YOUR EYE ON THE TARGET
- KEEP ON KEEPING ON

JI

BOLD GUTS STRATEGY – 8 DAY
PLAN TO IMPROVE LIFE!

ACRONYM STYLE DAY – 8

S – THIS IS SATISFACTION

IN THE FOLLOWING ORDER!!!!

- ENJOY WHAT YOU DO
- ALWAYS BE POSITIVE
- BE SATISFIED WITH WHO YOU ARE

JI

"IT IS NOT THE SIZE OF THE DOG IN THE FIGHT. IT IS THE SIZE OF THE FIGHT... IN THE DOG!"

MARK TWAIN (1835 – 1910)

"TO GROW TEACH YOURSELF AND LEARN HOW TO ALWAYS EXPECT THE BEST OF YOURSELF... *EVERYDAY!!!*"

JI

"MOST ALL CHALLENGES ARE SIMPLE, BUT...
NOT EASY!!"

JI

BEING YOUR OWN PERSONAL <u>LEADER</u>...

LIFE (**OF**)
EXPANDING
ATTITUDE
DISPLAYING
ENTHUSIASM (AND)
RESPECT

JI

119

"YES, YOU ARE SURVIVING BUT
THE TRUE QUESTION IS…
ARE YOU *THRIVING?*"

JI

"THANKSGIVING WILL HELP YOU GROW IF YOUR ARE *GIVING THANKS* EACH AND EVERY DAY AND YOUR THANKS ARE *BASED ON YOUR FAITH!*"

JI

"YOU CANNOT ESCAPE THE RESPONSIBILITY
OF TOMORROW BY EVADING IT TODAY."

ABRAHAM LINCOLN (1809 – 1865)

HOW YOU LOOK AT ROOM TEMPERATURE IS CRITICAL...

"MANAGEMENT IS LIKE A THERMOMETER, IT REACTS TO THE TEMPERATURE OF THE TEAM! LEADERSHIP IS LIKE A THERMOSTAT IT SETS THE TEMPERATURE OF THE TEAM!"

JI

"AS WE GET OLDER THE MONSTERS CRAWLED FROM UNDER OUR BEDS AND CREPT INTO OUR HEADS!!!"

JI

YOU SHOULD ALWAYS
COMMUNICATE BY <u>TWO</u>...

TALK
WITH
OPTIMISM

JI

FIND SUCCESS THOUGH V I C...

VISION
INTEGRITY
COURAGE

JI

YOU WIN WHEN YOU TAKE <u>ACTION</u>...

ATTITUDE (WITH)
CONSISTENT
TENACITY
INTEGRITY (AND)
OPTIMISM
NOW

JI

"GOD IS A SPIRIT, AND THEY THAT WORSHIP
HIM MUST WORSHIP HIM IN SPIRIT AND
TRUTH"

JOHN
4 : 24

THE PRAYER

IF WE STARTED OUR PRAYERS
WITH "THANK YOU"
INSTEAD OF "PLEASE HELP ME OUT",
THEN I'M SURE THAT THIS APPROACH
WOULD INCREASE OUR
STANDING AND CLOUT.

FOR YOU SEE OUR CREATOR GIVES US
CERTAIN THINGS TO HELP US OUT,
TO SEE WHAT OUR REACTION WILL BE
A HAPPY CHEER OR AN ANGRY SHOUT.

NOW IF WE TAKE THE BLESSINGS HE GIVES US
WITH A SMILE AND JOYFUL GLEE,
HE WILL MAKE SURE WE GET
MORE OF OUR WANTS,
JUST TRY IT OUT AND SEE.

FOR GOD IS TRULY A BENEVOLENT SOUL
WHO WOULD WANT US TO LEARN TO SHARE.
IF YOU DON'T WANT TO BELIEVE ME,
READ THE GOOD BOOK, FOR THE
STORY IS ALL RIGHT THERE.

NOW IF WE SHARE OUR WEALTH
AND LIVE MORALLY STRAIGHT,
FILL OUR HEARTS WITH LOVE,
INSTEAD OF BITTER HATE,
WE WILL SURELY GET TO MEET THE MAN
STANDING AT THE GOLDEN GATE.

SO, TRY TO REMEMBER THE NEXT TIME
THAT YOU KNEEL TO PRAY,
PLEASE BE GRATEFUL FOR THE
BLESSINGS YOU HAVE,
THE GOOD LORD WOULD WANT IT
THAT WAY!

JI

UNDERSTAND THIS SIMPLE APPROACH...

"EAT AN AVOCADO BEFORE YOU GO TO BED...
YOU'LL WAKE UP IN THE MORNING HAPPY IN
YOUR HEAD!"

JI

"IT'S AN AMERICAN OPPORTUNITY NOT AN AMERICAN DREAM!"

JI

"HAPPINESS IS LIKE THE SUN SET, IT IS THERE FOR ALL, BUT MOST LOOK THE OTHER WAY AND LOSE IT!"

MARK TWAIN (1865 – 1910)

"YOU SHOULD SAY TO YOURSELF I AM!
AN HONEST, INTELLIGENT, ORGANIZED,
PERSON, I AM ALSO RESPONSIBLE,
COMMITTED, AND A TEACHABLE PERSON.
ALL OF THESE COMMITMENTS HELP ME
GROW IN LIFE"

JI

"REFLECT UPON YOUR PRESENT BLESSINGS, OF WHICH EVERY MAN HAS PLENTY; NOT ON YOUR PAST MISFORTUNES, OF WHICH ALL MEN HAVE SOME!"

CHARLES DICKENS (1812 - 1870)

YOU WILL GAIN RESPECT WHEN...

"IN AND AT WORK YOU
COMPLIMENT THE ACTION...
NOT THE PERSON!"

JI

FOCUS ON THIS WITH <u>ACTION</u>...

ATTITUDE
CONCENTRATE (WITH)
TENACITY
IMPLEMENTING
OPTIMISM
NOW

JI

BE HAPPY WHILE YOU'RE LIVING, FOR YOU'RE
DEAD A LONG TIME

SPANISH PROVERB

YOUR MEMORIES WILL PROVE
THE FOLLOWING...

"GOOD FAMILY TIMES BRING OUT THE SUN!
WHEN THE GREAT FAMILY TIME IS DONE!"

JI

"WHEN YOU SHINE YOUR LIGHT ON OTHERS.
IT ALLOWS YOU TO UNDERSTAND AND GROW
TOWARD YOUR PASSION!"

JI

LUCK...
LABORING
UNDER
CORRECT
KNOWLEDGE

JULY 31

MOVE FORWARD IN LIFE WITH <u>GOALS</u>...

GETTING
OPTIMISTIC
ABOUT
LIFE
SYSTEMATICALLY

JI

TOUGH TO UNDERSTAND BUT TRUE...

"TRUE SUCCESS IN LIFE WILL COME FROM A SERIES OF CALCULATED RISKS!"

JI

WHAT IT TAKES TO BE A <u>WINNER!</u>

WILLINGNESS TO LEARN AND CONTINUE TO
EDUCATE YOURSELF.
INTEGRITY TO DO WHAT IS RIGHT ALWAYS
EVEN IF IT COMES SHORT   TERM PAIN
NEVER COMPROMISE THE INTEGRITY YOU
ESTABLISH. IMPORTANT AS   ONCE IT IS LOST
YOU WILL NOT GET IT BACK
NOW DON'T WAIT TAKE ACTION IN ALL
THINGS.
ENTHUSIASM FOR WORK, LIFE AND YOUR
PASSION. IT SHOWS AND IT IS CONTAGIOUS.
REMEMBER, WHERE YOU CAME FROM AND
WHERE YOU ARE IS THE RESULT OF MANY
HARD KNOCKS AND MUCH LEARNING.

JI

THEODORE ROOSEVELT
STARTED BUT I WILL FINISH...

"AS THE LEADER – THE BUCK NOT ONLY
STOPS WITH YOU...
IT STARTS WITH YOU TOO!"

JI

A GOOD COMPARISON...

"A BIRD SITTING ON A TREE IS NEVER
AFRAID OF THE BRANCH BREAKING,
BECAUSE HER TRUST IS NOT ON THE
BRANCH BUT ON IT'S WINGS.
ALWAYS BELIEVE IN YOUR WINGS AND... FLY!"

JI

"YOU NEED TO ***GROW THROUGH*** TIME…
DON'T **GO** THROUGH TIME!"

JI

THE BAD NEWS IS THAT THERE IS NOT
A KEY TO HAPPINESS!!!
THE GOOD NEWS IS...
IT ISN'T LOCKED!!

"YOUR REACTION TO A SITUATION
LITERALLY HAS THE POWER...
OF CHANGING THE SITUATION!"

JI

"STRIVE NOT TO BE A SUCCESS, BUT RATHER TO BE OF VALUE"

ALBERT EINSTEIN (1879 – 1955)

THE <u>SYSTEM</u> YOU NEED TO LEARN...

SETTING
YOUR
SUCCESS
THROUGH
EMOTIONAL
MOTIVATION

JI

"IN READING THE LIVES OF GREAT MEN, I FOUND THAT THE FIRST VICTORY THEY WON WAS OVER THEMSELVES. SELF DISCIPLINE WITH ALL OF THEM CAME FIRST."

HARRY TRUMAN (1884 – 1972)

YOU MUST UNDERSTAND AND LEARN THAT...

"TENACITY IS A CRITICAL SKILL
IN LEADERSHIP AS WELL AS
YOUR SUCCESS IN LIFE"

JI

HOW MUCH MONEY CAN YOU MAKE IN YOUR LIFE? "IT DEPENDS ON <u>DAD</u>...

DEMAND FOR WHAT YOU DO!
ABILITY TO DO IT!
DIFFICULTY TO REPLACE YOU!"

JI

"ALWAYS BELIEVE IN YOURSELF AND TRUST THAT YOU CAN MAKE A DIFFERENCE NOT ONLY IN YOUR LIFE, BUT IN OTHER PEOPLES LIFE AS WELL!"

JI

"IF ONE MAN PRAYS AND ANOTHER CURSES,
WHOSE VOICE WILL THE LORD HEAR?"

SIRACH
34 : 24

"BE KIND AND COMPASSIONATE TO ONE
ANOTHER, FORGIVING EACH OTHER, JUST AS
IN CHRIST GOD FORGAVE YOU"

EPHESIANS
4 : 32

YOUR JOY IN LIFE WILL GROW
WHEN YOU UNDERSTAND...

"TRUE FRIENDS ARE THE TENDER MERCIES
IN LIFE!"

JI

"WITHOUT FAITH IT IS IMPOSSIBLE TO
PLEASE GOD!"

HEBREWS
11: 6

PACE

POSITIVE
ATTITUDE
CHANGES
EVERYTHING

"WHEN YOU SHINE YOUR LIGHT ON OTHERS...
IT ALLOWS YOU TO SEE, UNDERSTAND, AND GROW TOWARD YOUR PASSION!"

JI

YOUR STYLE IN COMMUNICATION COUNTS...

"YOU CAN'T PUT YOUR FOOT IN YOUR
MOUTH IF YOUR MOUTH IS SHUT...
AND YOUR EARS ARE OPEN!
UNDERSTAND YOU LEARN AND GROW MUCH
MORE THAT WAY AND THINK BEFORE YOU
SPEAK!"

JI

"YOU NEED TO UNDERSTAND AS YOU GO THROUGH LIFE THAT COUNTING ON OTHERS TO HELP YOU ALONG THE WAY MOST OFTEN DOESN'T WORK OUT... UNDERSTAND PEOPLE ARE NOT AGAINST YOU...
THEY ARE FOR THEMSELVES!"

JI

LOOK INSIDE YOURSELF AND UNDERSTAND...

"YOUR GOALS AND VISION IN LIFE
SHOULD BE TO FOCUS ON YOUR
TALENTS AND WHO YOU ARE...
NOT WHAT OR WHO YOU
THINK YOU SHOULD BE...
DON'T COMPARE YOURSELF TO OTHERS!"

JI

FEAR
FALSE
EVIDENCCE
APPEARING
REAL

IF YOU WANT TO GROW IN
LIFE YOU NEED TO...

"FOCUS ON OPPORTUNITIES,
DON'T FOCUS ON PROBLEMS!"

JI

"DO WHAT YOU CAN, WITH WHAT YOU HAVE, WHERE YOU ARE."

THEODORE ROOSEVELT (1858 – 1919)

HOW YOU LOOK AT THINGS
IS WHAT COUNTS...

"YOUR VISION IS YOUR VISION,
YOUR CLEAR SIGHT OF THE VISION...
THAT IS WHAT IS CRITICAL!"

JI

"BEING TAKEN CARE OF IS **YOU**,
TAKING CARE OF YOURSELF!"

JI

3 - P'S - PRIORITIES OF THE <u>WORST</u> LEADERS IN BUSINESS....

POSITION
POWER
POSSESIONS

JI

THE ATTITUDE

YESTERDAY I MET A WOMAN
SHE MADE COOKIES THE SIZE OF A DIME.
WHEN I INQUIRED ABOUT HER HEALTH,
SHE SAID SHE WAS DOING JUST FINE.

SHE SAID THAT SHE WAS TRULY BLESSED,
TO HAVE ME ENTER HER LIFE AT THIS TIME.
I TOLD HER THAT IF A BLESSING WAS THERE,
THEN IT SURELY HAD TO BE MINE.

SHE TOLD ME THAT A GOOD ATTITUDE
IS THE GREATEST GIFT OF ALL.
WITH IT YOU CAN CONQUER THE OBSTACLES
WHETHER THEY ARE BIG OR SMALL.

SHE TOLD ME SHE KNEW OF
ONE GREAT TRUTH,
OUR MEETING WAS NOT HAPPEN STANCE.
FOR WHETHER YOU ARE YOUNG OR OLD,
WE ARE ALL PART OF THE BIG DANCE.

GOD IS PLAYING THE MUSIC,
AS WE GLIDE ACROSS THE FLOOR.
AND YOU MAY FIND A BLESSING,
FAR AWAY OR RIGHT NEXT DOOR.

BE KIND TO ANY AND ALL YOU MEET
IN THIS PATHWAY THEY CALL LIFE.
FOR GOD IS WATCHING ALL WE DO,
AND HE WILL TEACH YOU TO
DANCE JUST RIGHT.

JI

YOU CAN'T CONTROL OTHER PEOPLES ACTIONS YOU NEED TO UNDERSTAND...

"IF A BAD WORD ABOUT YOU GETS OUT...
LOOK OUT IT WON'T GO AWAY!"

JI

TWO SIDES OF THE COIN...

-   +

"FEAR   IS THE OPPOSITE OF   FAITH!"

JI

IN YOUR ENDEAVORS ALWAYS…
"BE BLESSED TO BE A BLESSING
HAVE YOUR THOUGHTS TURNING TO "GOD"
HAVE YOUR PATH REMAIN STRONG
HAVE YOUR ATTITUDE REMAIN HUMBLE
HAVE YOUR HEART FILLED WITH JOY AND
STRENGTH"

DIANNA HAUGEN

TRUE LEADERSHIP BOILS DOWN TO ONE WORD...

"IN LEADERSHIP, YOU HAVE TO BE
TEAM MINDED...NOT <u>ME</u> MINDED!"

JI

"REMEMBER NO ONE CAN MAKE YOU FEEL INFERIOR WITHOUT YOUR CONSENT"

ELEANOR ROOSEVELT (1884 – 1962)

"OUR DOUBTS ARE TRAITORS, AND MAKE US LOSE THE GOOD WE OFTEN MIGHT WIN, BY FEARING THE ATTEMPT."

WILLIAM SHAKESPEARE (1564 - 1616)

CONSUME WHAT YOU GET AT THE <u>LIBRARY</u>...

LEARNING
INTELLIGENCE
BY
READING
ALWAYS
RISING
YOURSELF

JI

"FOCUS ON...

DEDICATION, INTEGRITY, ACCOUNTABILITY,
THEN TAKE ACTION WITH COURAGE,
ENERGY, FOCUS, DETERMINATION,
AND SIMPLICITY, IT WILL BRING
RESULTS AND SUCCESS!"

JI

"YOU CAN NEVER STEP INTO THE SAME RIVER; FOR NEW WATERS ARE ALWAYS FLOWING ON TO YOU."

HERACLITUS
(GREEK PHILOSOPHER)

ALWAYS REMEMBER WHEN YOU
TRY SOMETHING NEW...

"IF YOU KNOW IN YOUR MIND
YOU GAVE IT YOUR BEST IN THE
EFFORT AND YOU PUT IN 100%...
REGARDLESS OF THE OUTCOME YOU
WILL HAVE SELF-SATISFACTION..."

JI

"A FAITHFUL FRIEND IS BEYOND PRICE;
NO SUM CAN BALANCE HIS WORTH"

SIRACH
6 :15

"TO FIND AND UNDERSTAND
HAPPINESS AND SUCCESS YOU NEED
TO COMMIT TO THE JOURNEY...
NOT THE DESTINATION!"

JI

HOW TO BRING <u>VALUE</u> TO YOUR CAREER...
VISUALIZE
ACTION
LEAD (BY)
UNDERSTANDING (THE)
EXPECTATION (OF OTHERS)

JI

"PEOPLE WHO'S BIBLES ARE FALLING APART...
ARE PEOPLE WHO ARE NOT...
FALLING APART!"

SANDRA PERKINS

THE BEST INDEX TO A PERSON'S
CHARACTER IS…
A) HOW THEY TREAT PEOPLE WHO
CAN'T DO THEM ANY GOOD AND…
B) HOW THEY TREAT PEOPLE
WHO CAN'T FIGHT BACK."

DEAR ABBY (VAN BUREN) (1918 – 2013)

"LIFE IS EXACTLY...
WHAT <u>YOU</u> MAKE OF IT!"

JI

ENJOY YOUR <u>FOCUS</u>...

FUN
OPTIMISTICALLY (AND)
CONSISTENTLY
UNDER
SPIRIT

JI

"THE TRUTH OF WHAT YOU
BELIEVE? TAKE A LOOK AT...
WHAT YOU ARE B-LIVING!
THAT WILL TELL YOU...
WHAT YOU B-ELIEVE!."

JI

"IF YOU ARE UPSET OVER SOMETHING WAIT
BEFORE YOU RESPOND...
EMOTIONAL PEOPLE MAKE BAD DECISIONS!"

JI

UNDER HEAVEN THERE IS NOTHING
IMPOSSIBLE. ALL YOU NEED IS
A PERSON WITH HEART.

CHINESE PROVERB

SIZE MAKES A DIFFERENCE, BUT NOT THE
WAY YOU THINK….
"IN ORDER TO STAND TALL, YOU
NEED TO GET SMALL AS HUMILITY IS
WHAT MAKES A PERSON GREAT!"

JI

UNDERSTAND WHAT BRINGS **IT** TO YOU IS ...
"IF YOU ARE HOPEFUL, CONFIDENT
AND CHEERFUL IN LIFE YOU
ATTRACT **IT**... **SUCCESS**!"

JI

"YOUR REACTION TO A SITUATION LITERALLY
HAS THE POWER OF CHANGING SITUATION!"

JI

TWO THINGS ARE CRITICAL….
"ALWAYS KEEP YOUR VISION…
IN THE STATE OF ACTION!"

JI

<u>TRUST</u> TAKES TIME BASED EXECUTING THE
FOLLOWING…
TRUTH – ALL TRUST COMES FROM HONESTY
AND OPENNESS!
RESPECT – RESPECT IS THE FOUNDATION ON
WHICH TRUST IS BUILT.
UNDERSTANDING – OF OTHERS,
PERSONALITY, STYLE, AND POSITION.
SUPPORT – SOMETIMES EVEN WHEN WE
DISAGREE
TIME – A GOOD THING IS, THE EBB
AND FLOW WILL BUILD ON ITSELF!

JI

YOU SHOULD ALWAYS REMEMBER...

"PEOPLE WHO ARE CONSISTENTLY
CONSISTENT, ARE THE ONES WHO
SUCCEED IN WHAT THEY DO!"

JI

"YOU SHOULD ALWAYS SAY TO YOURSELF I AM!

AN OPTIMISTIC, PUNCTUAL, ENTHUSIASTIC, FOCUSED GOAL SETTING, SMART WORKER! YOU WILL LEARN TO BE EXACTLY THAT"

JI

"THOSE WHO DON'T READ GREAT BOOKS ARE AT NO ADVANTAGE OVER THOSE WHO CANNOT READ!"

MARK TWAIN (1835 – 1910)

YOUR TEAM WILL BE BETTER
IF YOU UNDERSTAND...

"CONSISTENCY IS THE HALL MARK OF
TRUE LEADERSHIP! WHEN YOU ARE
CONSISTENT IT WILL DEVELOP COURAGE!"

JI

"GOD IS A SPIRIT, AND THEY THAT
WORSHIP HIM MUST WORSHIP
HIM IN SPIRIT AND TRUTH"

JOHN
4:24

"IF YOU ARE GOOD AT WHAT YOU DO ALWAYS
GO FOR THE OPPORTUNITY...
IF YOU FAIL IN THE ATTEMPT YOU CAN
ALWAYS GO BACK TO WHAT YOU WERE
DOING... SO WHAT DO YOU HAVE TO LOOSE?"

DAVE SHEELY

YOU ARE GARENTEED SUCCESS...

"IF YOUR <u>FAITH</u> IS LOCKED INTO YOUR VISION, IT IS IMPOSSIBLE TO FAIL!"

JI

"THE CERTAINTY OF MISERY, IS BETTER THAN THE MISERY OF UNCERTAINTY!"

BILL KEMPLE

"I AM A SUCCESS TODAY BECAUSE I HAD A FRIEND WHO BELIEVED IN ME AND I DIDN'T HAVE THE HEART TO LET HIM DOWN!"

ABRAHAM LINCOLN (1809 – 1865)

DOING WHAT YOU LIKE...
IS FREEDOM!
LIKING WHAT YOU DO...
IS HAPPINESS!

CHINESE FORTUNE COOKIE

EVERYDAY ...

"ALWAYS DO YOUR BEST,
TO BE YOUR BEST…
IN ALL YOU DO, THAT WILL
BRING YOU SATISFACTION"

JI

PLEASE LEARN YOU SHOULD...

"ALWAYS FOCUS ON IMPACTING OTHERS
IN A POSITIVE WAY AND ALONG THE
WAY YOU NEED TO UNDERSTAND...
EVERYTHING MATTERS!"

JI

"LIFE HAS NO REMOTE...
GET UP AND CHANGE IT YOURSELF!"

BOB MATTHEWS

IN **ALL** TYPES OF ATTITUDE...
ALWAYS
LOVE
LIFE
IT IS TRULY MAGICAL...

JI

6 WAYS THAT PEOPLE THINK
5 ARE BAD 1 IS GOOD...

5 BAD THOUGHTS
- MAYBE I WILL?
- MIGHT WORK?
- SHOUD HAVE!
- COULD HAVE!
- WOULD BUT!
1 GOOD THOUGHT
➢ MUST TRY...

JI

"SUCCESS IS NOT FINAL, FAILURE
IS NOT FATAL, THE COURAGE
TO PROCEED IS THE KEY."

WINSTON CHURCHILL (1874 – 1965)

THE 5 CENT MIRACALE

WHAT IS IT WITH KIDS AND A BAND-AID?
THE GREATEST MIRACALE CURE
CONCEIVED, FOR SCRAPES,
BUMPS, OR BRUISES, IT DOESN'T
MATTER WHICH,
IT WILL FIX IT BECAUSE THEY **BELIEVE!**

THIS PLASTIC STRIP, BELIEVE IT OR NOT
SPEWS MAGIC FROM ITS VERY PORES.
IF YOU ARE NOT CONVINCED,
WATCH IT WORK
WHEN A SMALL KID TAKES A
FALL ON THE FLOOR.

TO DREAM OF THE PERSON,
YOU WOULD LIKE TO BE
IS TO WASTE THE PERSON YOU ARE.
SO, CHASE YOUR DREAMS
FOREVER MY FRIEND,
NO MATTER HOW NEAR OR HOW FAR!

FOR THIS OLD WORLD GOES
AROUND AND AROUND
AND I AM SURE YOU WILL FIND,
THERE IS NO GREATER POWER ON EARTH,
THAN THE POWER OF YOUR MIND!

ALWAYS REMEMBER, WHATEVER YOU FACE,
ADVERSITY, DREAMS, OR DISPAIR.
YOU WILL MAKE IT THROUGH
JUST AS YOU WANT,
IF THE **BELIEF** IN YOUR HEART IS THERE.

SO, KEEP ONE AROUND TO REMIND YOU,
WHEN YOU FIND YOURSELF EVER IN DOUBT?
IF A 5 CENT MIRACLE CAN
WORK FOR A CHILD,
WE BIG KIDS SHOULD FIGURE IT OUT.

JI

WE ARE ALL BLIND IN A WAY...

"PEOPLE MISS THE TREASURES BEFORE THEIR VERY EYES, THEY IGNORE THE SMALL SATISFACTIONS AND THEY DO NOT ENJOY THEM AS THEY GO THROUGH LIFE!"

JI

SOME GOOD HABITS ....

"YOU WILL LEARN THAT HUMILITY AND
GRATITUDE ALONG WITH CARING OF
OTHERS, ARE THE KEYS TO MAKING
HAPPINESS LAST FOR YOU!"

JI

YOU ARE IN CHARGE OF YOUR <u>COURAGE</u>...

CONCENTRATION
ON
UNDERSTANDING
REAL
ACTUAL
GRIND
ENTHUSIASTICALLY

JI

"WHERE YOUR ATTENTION GOES, THAT
IS WHERE YOUR ENERGY FLOWS!"

JI

"YOU SHOULD SAY TO YOURSELF I AM!
A SOBER AND LOYAL PERSON, I ALSO
UNDERSTAND THAT I AM SELF EMPLOYED
REGARDLESS OF WHO SIGNS MY PAYCHECK, I
AM RESPONSIBLE FOR PRODUCING RESULTS!"

JI

"I CAN DO EVERYTHING THOUGH
HIM WHO GIVES ME STRENGTH"

PHILIPPIANS
4:13

"AS FOR ME AND MY HOUSE, WE
WILL SERVE THE LORD"

JOSHUA
24:15

"FAR BETTER TO DARE MIGHTY THINGS, TO WIN GLORIOUS TRIUMPHS, EVEN THOUGH CHECKED BY FAILURE, THEN TO RANK WITH THOSE POOR SPIRITS WHO NEITHER ENJOY MUCH MORE SUFFER MUCH, BECAUSE THEY LIVE IN THE GREY TWILIGHT THAT KNOWS NEITHER VICTORY NOR DEFEAT!"

THEODORE ROOSEVELT (1858 – 1919)

WHY I ALWAYS WEAR A TIE TO SEE MY
CUSTOMER?
"THERE IS NOTHING ABOUT MY
BUSINESS THAT I TAKE CASUAL!"

JI

"THE HAPPIEST MOMENTS OF MY LIFE HAVE BEEN, THE FUN WHICH I HAVE PASSED AT HOME IN THE BOSOM OF MY FAMILY!"

THOMAS JEFFERSON (1743 – 1826)

"YOUR ATTITUDE IS CENTRAL TO EVERYTHING IN THE SPHERE OF LIFE THAT YOU OCCUPY!!!"

JI

A GREAT PERSONAL MOTION...
"IT IS THE ACTION OF GIVING THAT
FEEDS THE SPIRIT OF JOY!"

JI

MOM'S 3 STEP PLAN TO OUR KIDS...

1) DON'T GET PREGNANT OR GET ANYBODY
PREGNANT!
2) GET MARRIED AND <u>STAY</u> MARRIED!
3) WORK HARD AND <u>TRUST</u> GOD!

MOM

DAD'S 3 STEP PLAN EXTRA CREDIT TO OUR KIDS...

4) GET A JOB AND START LOOKING FOR YOUR NEXT JOB THAT WILL TAKE YOU UP THE LADDER!
5) TAKE WELL THOUGHT OUT RISKS!
6) ALWAYS CONTINUE TO EDUCATE YOURSELF! DAD
**THROUGH IT ALL TRUST GOD AND BE GRATFUL FOR WHAT YOU HAVE...

(LOVE MOM & DAD)

GO TO <u>LUNCH</u> WITH THE CURRENT
INSPIRATIONAL PEOPLE...
LEARNING
UNDER
NEW
COOL
HEROS

JI

PIE PROCESS IN PROJECT MANAGEMENT...
PLAN THE PROJECT!
IMPLEMENT THE PROJECT!
EVALUATE THE PROJECT!

JI

"THE HEART OF A FOOL IS IN HIS
MOUTH, BUT THE MOUTH OF A
WISE MAN IS IN HIS HEART!"

BENJAMIN FRANKLIN (1706 – 1790)

Printed in the United States
By Bookmasters